BLUE
MORNING
LIGHT

Also by David Salner
John Henry's Partner Speaks
Working Here

BLUE MORNING LIGHT

POEMS & INTERVIEW
DAVID SALNER

POND ROAD PRESS
WASHINGTON, D.C.
NORTH TRURO, MA

Copyright © 2016 by David Salner.
All rights reserved.
Printed in the United States of America.

Cover art: Special thanks go to the National Gallery of Art in Washington, D.C., for permission to use *Blue Morning*, 1909, oil on canvas, by George Bellows, American, 1882–1925.

Book design and layout: Mary Ann Larkin and
 Patric Pepper.
Author photograph by Barbara Greenway.

ISBN: 978-0-9719741-7-3
Library of Congress Control Number: 2015953402

Further acknowledgments follow page 72.

Pond Road Press
Mary Ann Larkin and Patric Pepper
221 Channing Street NE
Washington, DC 20002
pepperlarkin@juno.com

Available through Amazon.com and other online booksellers, and through Pond Road Press.

This book is for Barbara, first and foremost,
and for Lily and Paul.

Dedicated to the memory of eight brave lives:
Mary Greenway, Pat Grogan, Stu Singer,
Becky Ellis, Tom Fiske, Frank Forrestal,
Priscilla March, Betsy McDonald.

CONTENTS

The Excavator

I. THE HEARTBEAT

Oil and a Stone	3
Metal-Black Feathers	4
Page-Turner	5
For Rose, Abandoned Daughter	6
After the Picnic	7
You Jerry Saxon and Me	8
Waxies	9
The Heartbeat	10
The Firehouse Dance	12
First Drunk—Baltimore	14

II. BLUE MORNING LIGHT

Of Brine and Hubbub	17
Pigeon Brave	18
Our Block	19
February Rain	20
Winter Island	21
Punishing the Night	22
A Sea Like This	23
The Path	24
Billy Sunday's Tent Revival	25
Brush Strokes for a Laundry Girl	26
Eternity	27

III. A PAINTER'S LIFE

Post-Impressionist Art	31
A Painter's Life	33

Osage, WV	35
17 Lines, Machines and Dreams	37
On a Photo of Babe and Lou	38
The Mystery of Rosebud	39
What Müntzer Said	40
The One After	41
John Clare Escapes the Asylum	42
Midnight to Eight	44

IV. SEA STAR

A Horn to the Rain	49
Homer's Advice	50
Shipwreck	51
The Gypsy Songs	53
Niko	54
Survival of the Sea Star	55
Final Jeopardy	57
The Denier	58
Dead Reckoning	59
A Dog by the Sea	60
An Author Interview	65

Acknowledgments and Biography

BLUE
MORNING
LIGHT

THE EXCAVATOR

> Based on the painting by George Bellows,
> *Blue Morning*, 1909.

Back arched
into a khaki brush stroke,
he swings a 4 lb. sledge and drives
a spike that pierces stone—by lunch,
blow after blow, he must sting deep enough
into the age-hard quartz to tamp a charge.
Then he will blow this rock into a breath
of glittering smithereens, a veil of grit
through which the sun will flare
on sweat, will wince through
tears, a nimbus of pain.

The sun gilds his back, reflects
off chunks and angles of the stone.
He surrenders to a trance in which his hand
suspends the hammer, like the load upon a crane,
rising with a hiss and rush of cables, a reeling in
of yesterday and yesterday, a lash of time,
until the present snugs against the gib,
balances in the morning light, this
moment, now, then the release,
the rapid fall of everything,
the full weight of the hours
plunging down.

I am the work, the raining down of it
upon the rock, the constant flow, the blood
that powers it. I am the rhythm of the hammer blow.
I am the sweat, the work I do, the life I lead.
I am this man, standing upon a rock
he will destroy.

I

THE HEARTBEAT

Oil and a Stone

for Julius Salner

You pick up a scythe and wipe the curved blade
until the orange rust
darkens with the oil's sweetness.
Then you produce a sharpening stone,
slide it in circles over the steel
as you beam and sway. "Careful,"
you breathe into my ear, as I finger
the razor-sharp edge. The air seems to breathe,
to wheeze with your breathing.

Grandma had a flower business,
sold armfuls of colorful petals
from a stall on the highway. Across the road,
the Cathedral of Tomorrow went up.
As the Baptists drove by,
she hawked sunflowers, roses on Sundays.
She fussed with her flowers
long after your death, survived you
by so many years my sister grew up
to remember her grandma, not you.

A life polished smooth, unknown.
Oil and a stone.

Metal-Black Feathers

"Don't play in your grandfather's sheds,"
they told my sister and me. So that's where we played—
among scythes and reels, pumps and blades,
carriage wheels, car wheels, come-alongs,
chainfalls, shackles, anvils—
among hundreds of pieces of tin and iron
sharpened or twisted in startling ways.

A Gypsy, tinsmith, ironworker, peddler—
he was a well-known performer of socialist dramas
for Hungarian immigrants. Back then,
we Hungarians were countless as grackles—
garrulous birds
with metal-black feathers.

The rest of his life
rusted in sheds.

One summer morning, he gave me a cardboard box
full of blocks of wood. I was six.
I fingered these treasures and asked:
"Can I hammer them together?"

"Tey're yours," he said, in his *tick* Hungarian tongue.
"No vun can tell you vat to do vit tem."
Then he walked into the house
and coughed his lungs away.

Page-Turner

for Edward Salner

I never guessed how tough you were,
until I sat beside you, all night long,
waiting. At least four times
I leaned over listening for the sound
of breathing, the sifting, the faintest
rattle of breath that would tell me
you were still on this earth, though you'd
become a man between worlds. Then I
fell back, wishing I'd picked up a good
mystery instead of this book of poems.
What I needed was a page-turner,
a story like the kind you used to tell,
about the night you and Uncle Vic
defended the store you worked in, in that
mill town shrouded in smog. A gang
came up from the river. You sensed
danger in their faces, so you
cracked soda bottles and waited—
weapons of glass in teenage hands—
as they drew nearer and you were eyeball
to eyeball. Then the lead guy nodded
and led his gang away, one by one,
all those tough guys into the smoke
of that Ohio town. About four a.m.,
I leaned over and found something better
on the bedside table, one of your last
favorites—I couldn't put it down.

For Rose, Abandoned Daughter

for Rose Cohen Salner

Sunlight streams through colored glass
blinding her as she bounces a ball
on a Persian rug. The game is like jacks,
only played with outdoor stones, which are
forbidden inside. So much is forbidden
inside a nice house. An old-world man
stares from a photo on the wall. His eyes,
haunting and haunted, tell her—*sit still,
little daughter. Back in the Old World,
we suffered. We sat still.*
She sits still.
It's August.
Smog drifts up the bay,
presses down on the port, the open-air markets
of Lombard Street, where chickens flap in their pens,
feathers no match for hard wood slats.
Debts not paid, never forgiven.
Meanwhile,
Rose has been waiting
all afternoon on the Persian rug.
Not quite perfect, this little girl,
she picks up the ball and bounces it, wondering
now, and now—
was it because she couldn't sit still
that the old-world man still hasn't come home?

After the Picnic

    My mother puts the blanket down,
      unwraps wax paper from our sandwiches,
releases the sweet and sour smells
    of lunch meat, dill pickles.

    My father leans against a tree
      with jigsaw bark, drinks something
purple from a glass, shakes another Lucky
    from the pack, cups his hands

    to light it, sighs the blue smoke
      in and out. His eyes meet mine.
I see through them into our future: a job lost,
    a long breakdown. After the picnic,

    he spirits me into the house
      on day-old sweat, on night air
that fills with wine, tobacco,
    the stale smells of his body.

    I breathe that richness
      when I need to know I had a father.

You Jerry Saxon and Me

I dreamed of that feeling I had as a kid
of running again and I mean fast
flying or falling down a long steep hill
in Baltimore near an old brick school
with an asphalt roof and an air-raid siren
I was feeling the summer wind in my hair
seeing the blur of pavement fly past
hearing the slap of Converse on concrete
nearing the corner of Duval and Chelsea Terrace
it was you Jerry Saxon and me
running again and I mean fast.

Waxies

They were bubblegum cards
wrapped in wax paper, pressed with an iron
so they'd skim over concrete, swallows on pond water,
and nestle against the brick walls
of PS 87. At recess we shot them, betting pennies,
all we had, kissing them, feeling the gloss,
the sweet slip of wax on our lips. Shoulder to shoulder,
we flipped them in a secret frenzy
like dice-rollers in night alleys. They were
ballplayers, mostly, or leather-faced generals
like Ridgway, MacArthur, or Migs and Sabres
engaging above a steel-blue horizon—
but my best shooter had the likeness
of a crowd standing over a box
containing something that must have been hands
because everyone in the crowd raised their arms
and their wrists spurted blood. Korea.
The back of the card explained. All spring
it sped over concrete, nosed into brick shadows, until
through some carelessness I don't remember
I lost it, returned to the cards I'd been ignoring,
to Jackie, The Duke, and Roy Campanella—
Campy, who had a tragic life
but played ball with such magic and love
I almost forgot the box full of hands.

The Heartbeat

Past the stone quarry and the sheer drop
of limestone, the white walls falling away
into the dark where the tiny men work
far below, past the grade school and a store
with a sign for Bortner's Lime and down
the Lincoln Highway to the Bentzel farm
and right on a road that follows a stream
through a patchwork of pastures and cuts
the earth into jagged banks, past the warped,
sun-weathered wood of outhouses
and flimsy barns—there, in that hayfield
just mowed, that kid, gripping the ball,
raising his arms in a stretch, stepping
forward, throwing hard at the boy
in his stance by a backstop of buff
straw bales, wagging his bat as the ball
streaks through the wild-onion smell
of spring air, like a comet with the tail
just a blur, until it slows in midcourse
and becomes a white thing in his sights,
so large he can count each red stitch
and see the neat weave, he can see it
that well, as he strides into it, his left
elbow trailing in the wake of his hips
until wrists roll the hands, the right
over left, and the fat of the barrel
connects, and he knows from the bright,
sharp crack that here in this field
no ball has ever been hit like that—
over the stubble in left and the lane
that serves as a property line, all the way

to a huddle of fawn-colored Guernseys
in the Meyers' cow lot—and the boy
with the bat in his hand and his eyes
still glued, feels something inside him
rising, a feeling that will last him
through all the tongue-lashings and worse
he'll get, that he has the power to hit
one over the property line and a good
ten yards into a new world where worry
is only a heartbeat from glory.

The Firehouse Dance

I played on a decent team, with Spike,
who could break any full-court press
by finding the open man, and Lucky,
who hit jump shots from beyond the arc—
but as athletes, pure-nerve-and-sinew stars,
Spike and Lucky were nothing compared
to Cheryl and Celeste at the Firehouse
Friday nights, as they beat time, pistons
of muscle driving heels in a stamp,
till Celeste picked up the rhythm with her
right hand, wagged it at me, at everyone,
glaring, come on and dance, I dare you,
come on, pulsating shoulder to shoulder,
kneading the air, shaping it, pushing it away,
leaning back, hips twisting, faces a blank
except for their scowling, eyebrows arched
in a hardness, in a unison of you know
and I know and we don't
give a fuck and the whole Firehouse
burning with those two volcanoes of anger
and desire, building up, as they linked arms,
shook shoulders and chest and Celeste
gave a bump, danced out
past arm's length and froze beyond flesh
and blood for an orbital moment, staring back
in a grimace suggesting only the end
of the song, and there's something worth
saying that hasn't been said—so they
started to tremble and stamp, to make sure
we knew there's something left, left out,
to shake with it, like fire, like rain,

they were liquid and gel, a shimmering
of water and heat, of hair and sweat
still seething . . .
                      When that dance was done,
Spike, Lucky, and I
chewed gum and waited for the next song.

First Drunk—Baltimore

"Pull over," I said,
pushed the car door open,
threw up on the walls of the Baltimore jail.
Southern Comfort, a little green schnapps.

I gazed at the walls towering into the night,
at the prison windows, whirling above me,
mere slits in the stone, and had the drunken thought
that a man inside the Baltimore jail
leaned on the same stone wall, pushing out
while I pushed in, holding my weight,
my hundred sixty whatever it was,
steadying it for a moment
of his long sentence.

Let a harbor breeze
blow the sweat from his brow, on these summer nights
thick as a wall. Let a port-weary ship
sound blues notes just for him, as it slips
through the soft waters of the Patapsco,
into the Bay, on one more trip to Rio.

II

BLUE MORNING LIGHT

poems based on the art
of George Bellows (1882–1925)

Of Brine and Hubbub

Forty-two Kids, 1907

Clowning on the dock,
glowing in the lights from shore,
naked, all splinters and bones, preening,
peeing into the summer night and prizing
the feeling that they shouldn't. Savoring
stolen smokes, they queue above this mix
of Hudson and the sea. They are the brine
and hubbub of the summer night. Boys,
diving in the oily darkness, floating
for awhile in heaven.

Pigeon Brave

Cliff Dwellers, 1913

I hardly notice anymore—because
the racket of the street is where I live—
but overhead, the sky is full of nightgowns;
pajamas; pristine, unearthly underwear—
sailing in the wind, on tarnished pulleys,
on ropes that coo to those who listen,
of the slip and slide of new-world days,
the reeling in of thank you and goodbye,
of memory—dove heavy, pigeon brave.

It's June. Warm breezes lift me in a race
of swirl and change, into a sky that's full
of laundry music, the endless washing of the air.

Our Block

Why Don't They Go to the Country for Vacation?
  lithograph of Lower East Side, 1913

Our block:
We've tried to put our mark on it—
which means we almost own it—stamping
and shrieking, so everyone will know we're here;
we fill the air with breezy laughter, ruttish groans; we
spread our lips and howl, or purse them, eyes closed, for
the world to kiss. We are more crowded here than any place
in India. Our faces press and pinch, from 10th Street to Canal,
into every column inch. That woman—I know every word she'll
say although her voice is lost in sound, rebuff and ricochet—
"I'd complain, but who would listen?" An agony of gestures,
a birdlike flight of hands, flapping into the air, attacking
sky, then falling back to nest on hips. My mom is there
with friends, hollering for me to come back home,
and I am running off with boys, from whom
I learn to never turn or blink, to keep on
running, to not look back.

February Rain

Men of the Docks, 1912

A ship is drifting up the river,
through the February rain, all the way from Hamburg

bringing work. A huddle of discouraged men
waits by the dock. Beside them, two white horses,

wanting to be put to use, soaked
from croup to withers. The men are fidgeting,

hands reaching through the rain-flecked air
for a barrel of orange flames.

I think I see my father—his hazel eyes
are searching through gray sheets of rain.

If I would speak and he would listen,
I'd tell him he was not to blame,

in this wide world, for anything.
If I would speak and he would listen.

Winter Island

Winter Afternoon, 1909

From the look of things today—
how scum and cinders tremble on the faintest stir
and rise of air—I'd say that gusts, by afternoon for sure,
will dash the island, whip trash and wrappers, thrash them,
river to river through the streets, down avenues. All night,
storm-slant will bury us in knives of ice, silencing
even gull-shriek and child-scream.

Tomorrow, at work, I'll look across the Hudson,
from this island, this vessel sailing into time,
above the settled waves, to the sheer cliff sides
of brick and mortar, of Jersey City, Hoboken.
Beyond my shift, through vent and hum,
through murmur of flue, rust-colored haze,
I'll glimpse the steep walls of the Palisades.

Punishing the Night

Stag at Starkey's, 1909

On Saturdays, at Sharkey's Club,
I chew cigars and watch the fights. All night,
a man with blue-white skin tries to embrace
a smoke-gray man. He strains to hold him up
and knock him down. With a surge
of power he pummels his mirror image
then freezes, a glimmer of ghostly skin
beneath the lights. By now they have quit listening
to the referee, their trainers, or the round,
thrusting an elbow, a knee, into a soft
pocket of life. Glistening like a creel
of still-live fish, they hug each other,
gloves flapping at kidneys, then punish
the darkness with a spasm of fists.

A Sea Like This

The Big Dory, 1913

Like frightened turtles, these sturdy men
hunch their necks into their collars,
turn inward, so they might find
shelter inside themselves—or an excuse
for not pushing the heavy dory out
into the wind. Maybe some repair undone,
the rigging still a tangle of rope
and icy brine. But they find no excuse,
and what they fear, that line of purple clouds,
still faces them. They know how thunderheads
emerge from distant hints, darkening breakers,
sweeping over them with sulks and shadows.
The sea will simmer and rise, exploding
from its bowl of shifting sand . . . But now,
these ruddy men have jumped on board
and rowed into the inlet, and from the look
on each red face, each face of these nine men,
they're hating every second in this wind
shifting to gale. Yet they've pushed off
as if so ordered. But who would order it,
who among us, to send nine fishermen
into a sea like this, to fetch a dollar home,
a dollar for their catch? We see them disappear
into a haze beyond our calling, as they ride out
upon a timeless swell. And our last sight
tells us not of any terror they might feel
but of a boyish inkling they've been caught
in the act of realizing, a little late:
This is something they should not have done.

The Path

Electrocution, 1917

His brow tilts upward
as he faces us, shoulders thrown back
against the chair, hands tightening
on the armrest, mouth agape
in the expression of a man
who has searched for something
and has to, finally, admit it's lost—

blindfolded, as if he were a mule
that might take fright, upsetting
the load of terror he must pull.

Eight dark-robed gentlemen
gather around him like the pages of a book
about to close.

One intones from a bible
last-minute instruction, offering
a path his soul can follow
who knows where.

Billy Sunday's Tent Revival

Billy Sunday, 1923

All summer, light towers blaze,
reflect off sweat. He glides across the stage
above us, lunges, thrusts finger, shoots words
like bullets at the good-for-nothing
wretches that we are; then sings
with overarching beauty
to that which lives in all of us,
the longing to heal ourselves,
ourselves, into the one and only
gift we make unto the Lord.
In a voice that trills among the pillars of the night,
he praises the mother of Moses as if she were
a neighbor lady, this humble woman
who was godly, who risked all
to hide her son from Pharaoh. "But Judas' mother
had no fear of the Lord, sure as I'm standing here,"
he yells—and the arrows that he speaks
seek us where we have fallen
on this sawdust floor, hiding
on hands and knees, wanting to be found.

Brush Strokes for a Laundry Girl

Little Girl in White, 1907

her hands, the rest of her will never grow into those hands—

her shoes are far too loose to play on stoops—

her skin is pale, white as the linen she collects—

she tosses our questions back at us—

she tosses her hair to have some fun—

the copper highlights, lost in Rembrandt shadows—

the words that cross her mind she crosses out—

she rolls her eyes—

she puts us on the spot—

her eyes burn through us—

she is the one who guides the brush.

Eternity

Blue Morning, 1909

A whistle stills the site, hushes
the whine and hum of cables.

Powder settles through the cyan light
into the quiet air of coffee break.

Someone tosses up a thermos,
which he catches in a blistered hand—

this man who sits upon the rock
he will destroy. He unscrews the top

and something swirls into the air,
heat vapors from a battered cup.

The stillness of this moment—
a mix of silica, a blur of fumes—

hovers above this crater
in the granite heart of town.

He sips the coffee, harsh and black,
the bitterness all his, tries to expand

this moment, savor the endlessness.
The whistle that will send him back to work

and break the day to shards of jagged light
seems an eternity away.

III

A PAINTER'S LIFE

Post-Impressionist Art

You got drunk and went to a museum
with two wonderful people, one of whose names
was Joshua, one of whose names
you have forgotten. We'll call her Tricia.
As for the museum, you remember
only Cezanne, cliffs that looked like houses,
houses that looked like cliffs. Then you walked back
to Joshua's and took off your shoes, while he
opened another bottle of rosé and Trish—
we'll call her Trish—reclined on the sofa. Her lips—
what can we say of those lips, which she
moistened and parted. You paused—
aware of your friend Joshua,
short and burly, at the far end of the couch,
raising his bushy eyebrows, two cats
arching their backs—
when Trish passed out. Cezanne, Van Gogh,
but what was Braque doing there,
among the post-impressionists? You held her ankles,
while Joshua grabbed her upper arms—
his hands hairy as tarantulas—and taking baby steps
you shuffled Trish into the bedroom
and placed her on the mattress
like two workman loading
a sack of fragile
goods on a truck,
                      and watched over her,
awed by the privacy of sleep and the soft
in and out of her breath.
                      Back in the living room,

Joshua poured two more glasses of rosé,
and you talked, with great authority,
about post-impressionist art.

A Painter's Life

A friend of mine is a painter,
but he turns metal for a living—
steel and brilliant titanium.

He puts the first piece of round stock
into the chuck and bumps it
until it runs out
to the plus or minus one-thousandth.
He thinks of the way he'd paint shadows
on a canvas he'd like to be working on.
Time passes.
A shift.
A life.

He locks up his tools
and opens a door on the night
full of people from Haiti to Pakistan,
all numb with work like he is.

He drives past the steps of the city—
fake marble, glimmering concrete—
and walks up three floors
to a glass of Shiraz.
A pool of magenta, a depth.

The sun glistens on brick facades
and white stone sills. The winter light
etches thin lines, drops shadows the color of asphalt.

Nothing changes—the same light
on stone and window glass,

the same city, plus or minus.
Nothing changes in this painter's life.

Osage, WV

A town of dust, broken windows,
and Scots Run, almost dry, running back
through years of torn-up tracks,

where we walk, now, past the shambles
of a diner and Toby's Ice Cream—
but Al's Shoe Repair is still there,

and Al himself bursts out
of the crinkled hide of the shop, his skin
steeped in the peppery tang of black polish

73 years. Behind him, a lode
of heels and soles, a brood
of answers crowding our questions, a crusher

of a handshake, and the great
cascading laugh falling endlessly
from a tipple of beamy teeth.

He talks about Saturdays
in the once and for all of this place
when a thousand people would shop,

pause to gossip, while a train
stopped to load at the mine. His eyes light up,
coal washed in sunlight.

"They've taken a lot from this town,"
he says of the train after train, "but don't count us out.
We're like Mohammed Ali, just doing our rope-a-dope

for awhile." We look back, and it's shift change,
again, the phantoms flooding past him,
carrying their lunch buckets home.

17 Lines, Machines and Dreams

The Gribetz Quilter was a horse of a machine,
    clattering away while I fed cotton
into its chatty teeth. I learned that machine
    from Gloria, a brute of a woman

with a happy face. And the Paragon Grinder
    was a smart machine. I ran it with Ron,
who cursed it, cursed everyone, while the machine
    danced Xs and Ys, diamond bits flashing

through coolant, whistling its light-metal song
    in the rain. Such a cheerful machine,
such an angry man. And chain-smoking Tom
    taught me the Lehman Lathe, a dinosaur

of a machine. Tom advised—like a jazz-man,
    the notes rustling deep in his lungs—
"Run it slow, man, be good to this old beast;
    you've got all midnight shift, so just

sit back and listen to the *clack-clack-clack*."

On a Photo of Babe and Lou

It has that 1930s look,
and they look like men of that time—
no more famous than I am.

Except for the baseball jerseys,
they could be two harvest hands
who wandered into a tavern
after tossing square bales in the sun.

The shade and the overhead fan
are good things to these men—
elbows resting on the bar, chaff
in their eyes, chaff in their hair.

"I might follow the harvest south
to Texas or California," Lou says.
"Hell of a life," Babe adds,
crow's-feet showing through his tan.

Lou puts a dime on the bar.
One more round for Babe and Lou
and the two harvest hands are gone.

The Mystery of Rosebud

On a tenth viewing of Citizen Kane

The screen fills with fire, and the heat
bubbles the varnish off the sled, but for one

flickering moment
Rosebud appears in the flames

licking the black and white screen
hungry as time. A workman tosses another load

of memories into the furnace,
which is where I am,

and darkness fills the theater.
A friendless death, a boyhood lost,

symbolized by the sled—I get those parts—but what
confounds me is the image itself,

how Rosebud was consumed by time,
and burned to nothing, and is gone.

What Müntzer Said

I thought of Thomas Müntzer
as I was making a list—

hamburger, diet cream soda,
bag of mulch, hearty

begonias, and I included
the phone number of an

insurance company, oh,
company, not co.

I added pills to the list,
the kind with a groove so you can

split them down the middle
like seasoned wood. Later that day,

a shower caught me
coming off the mountain. I heard

a clatter of rain on leaves, high up
in the canopy of hornbeam, hickory,

hackberry. The trees filled up
with rain, leaving me

wet to the skin. Müntzer said—
"All things have been turned

into property,
even the birds of the air."

The One After

I stumble over limestone,
slide down escarpments of yellow shale,
trample dead branches, ancient bones of memory
left from a winter of snow and dreams—crash into

a spring that was always shaping up,
looming above me, a mountain where I could be
hiking through maple and birch, entering
a rough wood realm, feeling my way

through stickers, low branches of hickory,
to emerge on the berm of a spring-fed pond
hefting sinkers, gray lead. How the sunfish
will greet me with an all-out aggression

of gold and green. High up and dime-like,
the sun warms a silent blue bell of sky.
The pond clouds with algae and water grasses.
Next summer passes, the one after passes.

John Clare Escapes the Asylum

(Mad English poet, 1793-1864)

John slips the greasy-shirted brute
who reeks of puke from those he's torn
and dodges chokehold large cold bang
of knuckle-bruise on socket bone

through yellow of hearth light dark hallway
runs to the blue glass evening glow
stoops to find a hand-sized key
and throws the bolt and sees the sky

ash-colored in a great round shell
of night the first in these four years
pauses to see the native air
flow softly through the wych elm tops

now laughs at lime trees he runs by
and has the thought that those thick trunks
have not been ripped by rich man's plow
dances through hazel scratch and laughs

at crunch of cob under his feet
as shadows wash his face with tartness
of crabapple of berry breath
the pleasant rot of spring-fed air

then sniffs a trace of charcoal sweetness
smoking on the chilly night hears gossip
low-voiced lyrical so near to ear
and strides into the clearing bold and shy

into the place where fires hiss gold
on Gypsy faces where eyes are shining
where all around the sugar of escape
to those that know so well the hate

on hate of the asylum that he fled he did
and song and honey-wine pick up
the heels of all the families there
a quick-limbed romp that dazzles him

their hands wake up in pools of dew
and shape the day from day-long love
and form a slow-horse caravan
to pillow his shrewd death.

Midnight to Eight

Midnight to eight I spend with machines,
with their incessant hum, the hubbub and scrape,
the snip-snip, the whine of well-oiled tongues
that winds through the night. I listen to lathes
go round, to mills that peck at each part-piece
like hungry birds, to grinders whose bit-sized
teeth make ultra-fine dust, golden iotas
drawn toward heaven by the drone of a fan.

I nod to this music and think of you
on a steep hill overlooking Morgantown
where you dream all night in your factory
of sleep, creating from each sweet breath
a new instant. Breathing in, breathing out,
working all night, making each now right.

IV

SEA STAR

A Horn to the Rain

Rain in the morning, so different
from drizzle in the pines at night.
At the glass door, my black dog
growls at nothing but the blur
of news, the slant of rain. She'd go
outside with me, to study
rain in veined begonia leaves,
green stems, a mix of blush
and blood. But no, old dog,
we'll stay inside and keep
the faith. A cup of French roast,
while Coleman Hawkins
squawks survival to the rain.

Homer's Advice

Athena disguised herself as Deiphobus, fooling Hector—
    I'm sorry, but mistaking a famous goddess
for your brother, that scene wasn't convincing. So Homer
    rescued it in live performances with a gesture
to the effect that on the day they handed out brains,
    the Prince of Priam wasn't first in line. The words
on the page weren't always that much, but Homer
    wasn't afraid to go over the top, morphing
galvanic as a fist-pumping, triumphal Achilles, or
    deadpan: his fans loved the lotus eaters,
the goofy smiles of stoned vegetarians, not to mention,
    "That plant is insidious—three of my men
tasted it and lost all desire for home"—*Ba-da-boom.*
    Lonely men, a boatful, is an Rx for laughter,
and the guffaws began with the sea breeze that brought
    the first notes (Homer twitched his ears
like a donkey) of those ooh-la-la women. As an old man,
    he took the stage each night, cane in hand,
the original madcap Blind Poet, breaking a leg
    or a line for a laugh or a cry. Afterwards,
he'd offer advice to poets and tellers, "Give the words
    pizazz, words are nothing without the *pizazz.*"

Shipwreck

He starves upon his lava perch. At dawn,
goes down to fight the tumble of the surf
in search of mollusks, scrambles upon a reef
bristling with coral blades. Blood from his cuts
leaks into the silver wash, oozes in a sinuous
stream that pulses with the waves, his salt
mixes with the ocean's endless
rise and fall of salt, his heart
awash.

**

Hunger is buoyant, rising inside him,
relentless, burning like acid, needle-sharp.
He dreams of succulent aloes, fruity kelp.
Wishes for them, wishes for a different island.
Here, all he can find are bitter mangrove.
They look delicious but are poison—
roots waving in the sea, tendrils
oscillating, rising with the tide
of hunger rising inside him.

**

Obsidian vistas
are valueless. He must decipher clues
that change before his eyes, must understand
traces littering the island
of myriad species. His target blurs,
specks roil, diminish in the crush of wind and sea.
He needs a hunter's eye, a language of gnashing,

teeth whetted by hunger. His weapon—
moonlight splintering like glass.

⁎⁎

He's mapped each cliff and outcropping
and found few crevices where flesh can hide
but this afternoon he just discovered
in the shelter of a ledge, this nook,
a tiny darkness
full of tenderness,
fluttering with life.

The Gypsy Songs

for Ian, Kayla, Nathaniel

I walk from the forest toward the campsite
and hear a wisp of Dvorak dying out.

The campfire explodes with a rush
consuming the brush we gathered all afternoon
to ignite the split logs.

Why does Nathaniel's violin
make me cry at the edge of the darkness?

I've come back into that ring of light.
He is playing *The Gypsy Songs*.

**

After sunset the horse-flies stop biting.

The children come back to us
from the blacktop roads of the campground.

The woods darken
across this leafy ridge of mountain.

Aspen and hickory loom over us,
shadows moored in soft waves of twilight.

We sit by the fire, drinking, whispering,
while they fall asleep, listening to us.

A mosquito purrs in its kingdom of darkness.

Niko

I can't imagine life through the eyes of a goat,
but there is a boy who says that Niko
needs a window.

It's autumn.
The orange scent of Grand Marnier
vanishes into the chilly night.

and Niko sleeps in a white shed,
the flat yellow eyes finally closing, the short legs
folding in the straw under the weight

of a round belly.
The first cool night, the orange scent.
The boy who knows him, who knows him

as he knows himself.
Who says that Niko
needs to see the horses, who sleep standing up

at the edge of a steep field.
Needs to see them
through a window I would make for him.

Survival of the Sea Star

"Whoa," you say, and point
past the splintered shells, bits of coquina,
to a sea star—black underside, a trim of copper scales—
upon the wet, gray wash. I take the picture,
you toss it back.

We walk back across a spine of dunes,
push through a tide of wind,
back to a house on stilts, sit on the porch,
in chairs of heckled wood, our skin
still blazing with the winter wind.

I pour shots for us, cheap scotch.
A sea star isn't fragile, you tell me, its arms
pry clams apart, break tight hinges—and this
is the amazing thing—the way their bellies prowl,
harvesting a sweetness from the shell.

We gaze into a haze, a faintness
seething in the sun. I pour two more
and think of work I've done, of oceans tended—
of sizzling steel, blood-red magnesium. The furnaces ran cold,
filled with the ice of time.

The sea star is a belly-wanderer, survives
a century of filth, while muscling through
oil spills, DDT, raw sewage,
used syringes, and the wasted fuel
from the navy's fleet of nuclear subs.

Tomorrow, the sun will shadow everything
of wave and sand. We'll hike into the wind,

which carves us into something
we can't see, can barely feel, must sense
as we drift down the beach, are swept along.

Final Jeopardy

More than anything you love to
put up your tired feet and watch
Jeopardy in the evening with Lily
and the dog and the darkness
resting outside on the boards
of the deck and a pointed or
wounding remark to which you
answer what is a barb by clicking
a ballpoint pen for your buzzer
as the other contestants are stumped
the librarian and the software
specialist from the West Coast
where you never lived and the
darkness moves in the trees
beyond the deck warning you
not to bet it all save something
the leaves sigh for the long ride
home as you stare back through
the bus window and people in
Texas watch you go by and whisper
words that will follow you forever
why didn't you know why didn't
you answer to a dance in triple
time and a jacket what is bolero?

The Denier

There was a man who denied the grass
under his feet and the birds descending
from the great sky to roost on the graves
and the graves he denied the graves
and no to the skulls of another time
precisely because they were from
another time and no to the smoke
twisting from the stacks and no
to the fire in the furnaces even though
an ember breathed gray and red
beneath a whisper red and gray
and no to the birds he denied
even the grass upon the graves.

Dead Reckoning

I stop for directions at a store
where all the light in the world seems to gather
against the night I've been lost in. The clerk
puts his finger on the map at a point
where the blue roads radiate, like veins

too frail to carry me. His skin is ashen
from long hours worked under florescent light.
He stops to unlock a cabinet for Marlboros,
extra long, and I think back to when I smoked.
According to Galeano, the Cariri Indians

discovered tobacco so they could talk with God,
which this customer needs to do in a hurry
from the way he rips at the cellophane.
Not the taste or smell but the moment
of inner peace when the phosphorous explodes

and you squint in the blue-gray smoke
and suck in a spiritual force
that gives you the power to hold everything
in abeyance. At a certain point in my life,
I knew I had what I'd always wanted, which didn't mean

I could ever stop wanting, because wanting
had become continuous, almost soothing,
unplumbable, like the strumming of the sea.
I roll down the window and listen
for the waves coming in, the syllables

of what I most want, guiding me
by my longing, breaking far out.

A Dog by the Sea

Just after dawn, we get up,
without coffee, and let the dog lead us
through a grove of wind-stunted trees,
spiked succulents, red-berried holly,
and over the dune ridge out of the gray
of still sleeping minds. A line of pink
from the not yet risen sun
reminds me of the lilac shadows
caught in the radial grooves of shells.
I take up your hand and feel the blood
warming your fingers, as the dog bounds off
dragging her leash through wet sand.
She's after gulls and a line of waves
that repeat themselves, she seems to think,
because they want to play.
                                          A morning breeze
stirs the now turning tide, breathing over it,
sighing toward bayside. As the waves come in
whorls of light unfold on the sand. How I want
for us to repeat ourselves, on and on,
you holding the leash of a silly dog, me
feeling the beat, the blood in your hand.

AN AUTHOR INTERVIEW

PRP: What have been the greatest influences on your writing? How have these influences changed over the years?

DS: The first influence is industrial labor, the jobs I worked at for 25 years—and the coworkers who taught me difficult and hazardous trades—or tried to. I never was a quick learner.

The workplaces offered vivid imagery: the loneliness of a machine shop on night shift; a furnace of molten steel, yellow-white and sizzling; or molten magnesium with its blood-red glow; or an old mining town, abandoned except for a few lonely shops.

Our jobs—even the mind-deadening ones—arm us for creating literature as we learn to devote care and thought to our workplaces, and to appreciate the colorful characters who live there. Where did Melville get the images for Bartleby or Moby Dick if not from experience as a worker low on the pecking order?

He knew jobs that reduce humans to near-automaton status as well as thrilling maritime adventure. Twain was a riverboat captain, Whitman a housebuilder and volunteer nurse. Occupational influences abound in the pages of these writers. If I ever have the time I'll write a book of essays on this topic. (That's a hint for anyone disbursing grant money.)

I've written about the world of layoffs and bruised knuckles, but I don't think we should submit to the notion that the bruised knuckles of the oppressed, in themselves, equal literature or that we have little to learn from studying the craft of great writers of the past, even though that list may include a few blockheads and scoundrels.

"Machines and Dreams" and "Midnight to Eight" are machine-shop poems, so I'm not finished with manual work as a topic. The brooding presence of the mines, the brutality of sweeping layoffs, which always seem to happen just before Christmas—some experiences will always be with me. But in the leisure of retirement, I'm attracted to other areas, as well. It's a treat, for example, to set your imagination free on everyday artifacts, as in "A Photo of Babe and Lou," or to become caught up in the vision of great artists like George Bellows and Francisco Goya.

The last poems in this book come under the influence of a different mood. Love that deepens in old age is satisfying while at the same time awakening a longing for more than is possible in life. A mixed blessing, maybe, but one that I am very fortunate to experience. That this mood should occur in my writing surprises me, and it's one of the ways that my wife, Barbara, and daughter, Lily, have left their imprint.

PRP: You mention several great nineteenth century and early twentieth century writers and artists as influences—Melville, Whitman, Twain, Bellows, Goya. In correspondence with PRP you've mentioned Philip Levine as a poet whose work you admire. How has Levine's work influenced your work? Are there other contemporary poets whose work has informed your work, either thematically or formally, or both?

DS: Thanks for trying to bring me up to date, Patric, and yes, Levine was a big influence. I was working in a machine shop when I noticed his book *What Work Is*. I was surprised to find that someone could write about factory experiences in such an interesting way. My early poems were influenced by his, but more importantly his work *encouraged* me.

Now, when I reread *What Work Is* or *The Simple Truth* it's more to get a sense of the way stories can be recounted with such a lively humanity, often through small details. In the poem "Bessemer" he remembers years earlier going to sleep in a desolate rail yard and waking up to find that one of the rough characters that roam such areas had stood over him during the night but spared him. The proof is the cigarette he or she left behind. This object tells Levine that he was meant to live—"But how / and why I was still to learn."

Dorianne Laux is another poet with a working-class background. She has a refreshing iconoclastic humor. You have to be convinced that you know a thing or two, based on experience, to say some of the things she says. Actually, a lot of people say those things, but few say them so well in poetry—and make you laugh. Isn't humor undervalued in poetry today?

Don't poets have to be artists of experience? Can we write convincingly while at the same time entertaining postmodern or post-postmodern doubts about our shared reality? Doesn't our trust for loved ones—as well as doctors, airplane pilots, coworkers, other drivers on the highway—doesn't this trust argue against today's craze for edgy, ambiguous literature? Don't forms of experimental writing become dull when they set out to toy with that trust?

I have more to say about these issues, but I'd be interested to hear what you and other poets think of them. Do you think you could include my e-mail address dsalner@yahoo.com?

PRP: We can certainly print your e-mail address here in this interview. Be sure to let me know what kind of feedback you get and conversations you have!

You mention Levine's fondness for narrative, and allude to the more edgy and ambiguous poetry in many journals today. It would seem that narrative well done is the opposite of the ambiguity I think you mean. Your narrative poems carry the reader along with unbroken ease, often into poignancy. When did you first begin writing narrative poems? Was it a conscious choice to use narrative or did your poetry just morph naturally into narrative?

It wasn't a conscious choice. Friends and coworkers have told me wonderful stories that reflect who they are. But the way they speak—tone, timing, facial expression, hand gestures—doesn't translate into literature except through a lot of reimaging. How voice and character are conveyed is all-important.

Poetry has a longer history than prose, especially as narrative. The poetic line is a shorter unit than the prose paragraph or chapter, but the poet in the free-verse age has a great opportunity to decide what it represents at each moment of a character's story. The movement from line to line can add expectation, tension, and poignancy. And thanks for seeing that in my poems.

Edwin Arlington Robinson was a master of narrative poetry. His small-town world of nostalgia and wrecked lives—a country-western world—is based on a pessimism I don't identify with. But I admire the way he presents both main characters and bystanders. The brutal ending of "Richard Cory" reminds me of the suicidal episodes of today's stars and other violent acts of despair we see around us, although it was written more than a century ago.

I think I see an implied question in your comment about ambiguity, and I'll try not to dodge it. Ambiguous images are often the end result of our search for meaning and beauty. Writers like Levine and Malamud often crown a narrative with a wonderful open-ended conclusion. Some of today's writers go further and eschew straightforward narrative and closure. But doesn't closure exist, in art as in life? Human beings confront ambiguity at every turn, but should we fetishize it? Shouldn't we strive for clarity?

PRP: Why do you feel it's important to defend a straightforward narrative poetry of clarity and closure against a more ambiguous poetry of multiple meanings and uncertainties? Don't both have a place in contemporary poetry? What are their roles given the current literary scene?

Both types should be defended. I like the William Carlos Williams poem with the lines—"It is difficult / to get the news from poems / yet men die miserably every day / for lack / of what is found there." He was a doctor and saw many people die miserably, and he cared.

All of us care. We care about each and every story woven into the social fabric. Stories. And narrative is what brings them to life, narrative is the art, it's what turns a still shot into a movie (and of course still photographs and paintings also tell stories). Narrative dictates what words are chosen and how one line follows another.

Some great stories turn on an image that we will never understand. In my poem "The Mystery of Rosebud" I look at the image in Orson

Welles' great film, *Citizen Kane*. What does Rosebud mean? We're fascinated by it because of its possible meanings and uncertainties.

To the workmen who come across Citizen Kane's sled, it's just rubbish for the fire. That's the final irony, and it's a powerful one. In fact, however, many workers *do* pause over such objects and pause to wonder about them: why did a man with millions of dollars' worth of collectibles and fine art save this ordinary kids' sled? What did it mean to him?

The stories of ordinary working people contain unexpected meanings. Literature today is a little more concerned with hidden lives than it used to be. The lives of black people and women have an extra power when told now because they were so long repressed. And the repression continues. But how much is written about those who work with their hands, including African-American and female laborers? My aim is not so much to expose the social wrong involved in this—which would be old news—but to look at the extra layer of meaning it represents. In my poems "A Painter's Life," "17 Lines . . ." and "A Photo of Babe and Lou," I tried to introduce subtleties based on the fact that the humanity of working people is still a secret.

I try to connect when I write. My audience starts with my wife, my daughter, and coworkers—past coworkers since I just retired—and includes others. My wife and daughter will actually read my work, and I'm thankful for that. For them, a simple story, well told, is sometimes sufficient. But they also hunger for stories that take up life's mysteries and ambiguities. Don't both kinds of stories need to be told?

PRP: Let's turn now to your new book, *Blue Morning Light*, which is anchored by a sequence of ekphrastic poems based on the work of the 20th century American painter George Bellows. The book is titled after one of his paintings. In light of what you have said about experience being the fount from which your work springs, what would you say is the influence of other arts on your poetry? How do such arts as painting, sculpture, music—acts of the imagination—inform your poetry?

Painting has always interested me, even in childhood. A close friend of my parents, an Austrian refugee, was a great painter. Her name was Eduarda Lynn, which doesn't mean much to anyone, but I mention it to give her a nod. Of which she got precious few during her life. Recognition is fickle at best. I grew up watching Eddie and my father paint. Today, our living room features her paintings and looks like an Eduarda Lynn gallery.

I was deeply impressed by how alive Bellows was to life around him. He painted in New York and loved the Lower East Side, which is an area I lived in for a time. When Bellows painted its stoops and streets it was the most crowded spot in the world, with more people per square mile than Calcutta or Shanghai. He was impatient with snobs but loved crowds. Or so I see his paintings.

His paintings and drawings provided me with a way to take up crowds and the life of individuals within them. His *Men of the Docks* shows a group of men looking for work on the waterfront. I had no trouble imagining their mood from my own experiences in unemployment lines. The poem that finally emerged, "February Rain," includes a dejected father, as well, my own father. His life included some failure.

"A Horn to the Rain" references jazz musician Coleman Hawkins, as well as our dog, Sugar.

Experience is a strong influence in both the creation and perception of art, and we should welcome that. Some people try to produce art out of thin air, but the result is thin art.

PRP: The action of your poetry takes place in a variety of geographical settings, places where you once lived. You mention, for instance, that you lived for a time in the Lower East Side, the setting for many of the Bellows paintings and your poems after those paintings. How is your sense of place important to your poetry, particularly the poems included in *Blue Morning Light*?

I'm fortunate to have lived all over the country. I spent part of my childhood among the creeks and farms of southern Pennsylvania and another part in Baltimore. "You Jerry Saxon and Me" and

"Waxies" are from the city and "Heartbeat" is from the country. My adult life, until relatively recently, was nomadic. I lived in desert, high plains, frigid far north, green West Virginia mountains.

Writers want to treasure an environment based in nature during a time when we're so aware of nature's destruction because of the way society is organized, which is a threat to nature *and* humanity. This goes back to the response by the Romantic poets to the industrial revolution and continues today in the work of fine nature writers like Rick Bass.

Because George Bellows painted the crowded streets of the Lower East Side or construction sites he was called an "ash can" painter. Though his seacoast paintings show that he had a wide-ranging imagination, he was at his best as a city painter, whether or not he painted a single ash can.

I lived in the Lower East Side for a few years during a time when it was still a slum. Bellows' paintings stirred me to write about this area. But more important to the writing of "Excavator," "February Rain," "Eternity," and others is the influence of the workplaces and coworkers. The workplace is a subsection of the city, with its own liveliness. And the city and the workplace won't always be viewed as destructive forces.

I hope it's not too much of a leap to quote Whitman on language and the source of its richness: "Its final decisions are made by the masses, people nearest the concrete, having most to do with actual land and sea."

PRP: Thank you, David, for all of your thoughtful answers. One last question: You mentioned during correspondence with PRP that you were involved in the civil rights and antiwar movements in the 1960s. You also return, both in your poetry books and in your answers here, to the influence of the workplace and coworkers, and to the injustices you have witnessed firsthand during your life.

In the 1960s, Martin Luther King said, "The arc of the moral universe is long, but it bends towards justice." Considering all

you have witnessed over the course of your life in the mines and factories of America, as well as what we see on the evening news, do you agree with his statement? If so, then what would you say are the forces that bend that arc?

I agree with the way you pose the question more than the way King posed it, because justice isn't inevitable. Considerable social force is required. The movements around Black Lives Matter and Fight for $15 and a Union are very good beginnings. But from what I've seen and experienced justice won't come under the current social system.

Social struggles that point in the direction of a society based on human solidarity have a liberating effect in all areas, especially literature. The expansion of democratic rights during the era of the Civil War led to the sweeping vistas of Whitman, Melville, and other great writers of that period. And just think how miserable American literature would be today without the sweeping democratic perspectives introduced by the black rights and women's rights movements.

Writers have a great role to play. Like everyone else, we can join the protests. And we should study the rich lessons of past social struggles. And of course we should produce the best literature we possibly can—not necessarily protest literature, which isn't always of high quality.

Writers have a selfish interest in democratic rights. We don't want to have our freedom of expression closed down, and we shouldn't want to see that happen to others. I respect what writers do, even those I most disagree with. Because the effort to produce art and literature shows confidence in humanity. And something else: the creative life that writers are committed to will come to fruition when culture is the property of all the world's citizens.

ACKNOWLEDGMENTS

Thanks to Patric and Mary Ann for support and skillful work, to the Dr. Henry P. Page Laughlin Foundation for their 2014 award, and to the editors of the following magazines where these poems previously appeared, some in slightly different form and some under different titles.

Amoskeag: "After the Picnic"
Atlanta Review: "Homer's Advice"
Delaware Poetry Review: "The Firehouse Dance"
DMQ: "The Denier"
Drafthorse: "Midnight to Eight"
Evansville Review: "First Drunk—Baltimore"
Gray's Sporting Journal: "The One After"
Heron Tree: "Oil and a Stone"
Hamilton Stone Review: "A Sea Like This," "Shipwreck," and
   "You Jerry Saxon and Me"
Hawaii Pacific Review: "Eternity"
Innisfree Poetry Journal: "The Excavator," "On a Photo of
   Babe and Lou," and "Page-Turner"
InPosse: "The Mystery of Rosebud"
Iodine Poetry Journal: "Metal-Black Feathers"
Irish Literary Review: "Winter Island"
Kestrel : "Osage, WV"
Magma, UK : "Pigeon Brave"
Moth, Ireland: "The Gypsy Songs"
New South: "A Dog by the Sea"
North Dakota Quarterly: "Waxies"
Pedestal: "Post-Impressionist Art" and "Survival of the
   Sea Star"

Poet Lore: "The Heartbeat" and "Punishing the Night"
Poetry Daily: "Final Jeopardy"
Poetry East: "Niko"
Quiddity: "Dead Reckoning"
Rappahannock Review : "Billy Sunday's Tent Revival"
River Styx: "17 Lines, Machines and Dreams"
Salmagundi: "Of Brine and Hubbub"
Saranac Review: "Our Block" and "The Path"
Slant: "John Clare Escapes the Asylum"
Tar River Poetry: "A Horn to the Rain"
Threepenny Review: "Final Jeopardy"
Tupelo Quarterly: "February Rain"
Verse-Virtual: "A Sea Like This," and "February Rain" under the title "Men of the Docks"

BIOGRAPHY

David Salner's writing has appeared in Thr*eepenny Review*, *Iowa Review*, *Prairie Schooner*, *North American Review*, *River Styx*, *Salmagund*i, *Poetry Daily*, and many other magazines. His first book, *John Henry's Partner Speaks*, was published in 2008 and his second, *Working Here*, won the Rooster Hill Press competition and was published in 2010. He worked for 25 years at manual trades, as an iron ore miner, steelworker, and laborer. He has also worked as librarian and teacher. He has received grants from the Dr. Henry P. Page Laughlin Foundation, the Maryland State Arts Council, and The Puffin Foundation, and was also the recipient of the 2009 Oboh Prize. Garrison Keilor performed one of his poems on NPR. His writing has been nominated three times for the Pushcart Prize and once for a Best of the Net award.

COLOPHON

The font used for titles in this book is P22 Wedge, designed by the renowned New Zealand architect Bruce Rotherham. Rotherham became inspired as a young man by Herbert Bayer's "universal alphabet," created at the Bauhaus in 1927. He began in 1947 to work toward creating and refining his Wedge alphabet. It was not to be commercially released until P22 Type Foundry did so in 2014.

The body text of this book is set in Minion Pro, an Adobe Original font designed by Robert Slimbach. Inspired by classical typefaces of the late Renaissance, Minion is a highly readable typeface, which combines modern sensibilities with deep-rooted elegance, beauty with functionality, and versatility with old-style elements.

This book was printed by Lightning Source Incorporated in the United States of America.

www.ingramcontent.com/pod-product-compliance
Lightning Source LLC
Chambersburg PA
CBHW032132090426
42743CB00007B/572